Praying
with the
Psalms

Praying
with the
Psalms

3-Minute Devotions for Lent and Holy Week 2025

SHANNON WIMP SCHMIDT

Ave Maria Press AVE Notre Dame, Indiana

Nihil Obstat: Reverend Monsignor Michael Heintz, PhD
                 Censor Librorum

Imprimatur: Most Reverend Kevin C. Rhoades
                 Bishop of Fort Wayne–South Bend
                 Given at Fort Wayne, Indiana, on 19 August, 2024

The *Nihil Obstat* and *Imprimatur* are official declarations that a book or pamphlet is free of doctrinal or moral error. No implication is contained therein that those who have granted the *Nihil Obstat* or *Imprimatur* agree with its contents, opinions, or statements expressed.

Founded in 1865, Ave Maria Press is a ministry of the United States Province of Holy Cross.

www.avemariapress.com

Paperback: ISBN-13 978-1-64680-379-8

E-book: ISBN-13 978-1-64680-380-4

Cover image © Gettyimages.com.

Cover and text design by Christopher D. Tobin.

Printed and bound in the United States of America.

*To Eric, the best husband in the world,
for putting up with my complaining every Lent
and loving me like Jesus every day.*

Introduction

Year after year, Lent gives us a chance to grow in our relationship with the Lord through daily disciplines, sacrifices, and prayer, which free us for spiritual renewal. One of the simplest ways to spend more time allowing the Lord to refresh our spirits is by slowing our pace and quietly meditating on God's word. This devotional gives you a simple structure for contemplative prayer that is built upon the liturgical psalms of the season.

The psalms have always played an important role in the prayer of God's people, from the time of King David to the present day. These hymns of ancient Israel express timeless truths about the human relationship with God and give voice to many of our common emotions and experiences in the spiritual life.

In the Catholic Church the psalms also form the rhythm of our liturgical life. We sing or pray responsorial psalms at every Mass. Religious communities, clergy, and many laypeople recite psalms daily as they pray the Liturgy of the Hours. The psalms shift by days and seasons in each of our liturgies, and the Lenten psalms speak particularly of penitence, conversion, and trust in God. These psalms form the backbone of our reflection and prayer in this devotional, providing the rhythm and structure of our own Lenten transformation.

Each daily devotion begins with a meditative phrase that is repeated throughout the week and a recitation of a psalm verse from the Lenten responsorial psalms. A brief reflection sparked by the psalm text will follow. Next, you will be invited to a short spiritual practice based on the reflection, and finally, the devotion will close with a brief contemplative prayer, anchored in the opening psalm verse.

Silence is a particularly important part of these devotions. If you're uncomfortable with silence, try simply setting one minute aside before beginning each meditation to enter more fully into the prayer. If silence is a regular practice for you, there is room for a period of extended silence after each section of the meditations. Keep in mind that there's no right or wrong way to use this devotional. It's meant to be an aid for you to create space for personal encounter with Our Lord and to contemplate the majesty of God's presence.

I pray that this little book is a blessing to you. This season is a powerful time to reconnect with God and rediscover God's tender mercy. It is an honor and a privilege to walk with you in these forty days of Lenten fasting, discipline, and prayer. I pray that you will draw closer to Jesus and find in him all you ever desire.

Ash Wednesday

† Create in me a clean heart, O God.

"I acknowledge my offense, and my sin is before me always" (Ps 51:5).

Most of us would not consider ourselves bad people. We live ordinary lives, trying to be kind, even if we occasionally fail. In the everyday routine, it's easy to gloss over our shortcomings compared to others' glaring sins.

Yet Ash Wednesday calls us to acknowledge what our sins truly are: moments when we decided our will was more important than God's love. We admit that we are actually no better than anyone else. We are sinners who need Jesus to save us. The ashes on our foreheads mark us publicly. We cannot deny the truth. Jesus, show me my sins and how it is you want to free me.

Sit in silence with the Lord.

Where in your life do you need God's mercy and forgiveness? Invite Jesus to transform that place through his tender mercy.

† "I acknowledge my offense, and my sin is before me always." Lord Jesus, have mercy on me. Amen.

Thursday after Ash Wednesday

† **Create in me a clean heart, O God.**

"Blessed the one who follows not the counsel of the wicked . . . But delights in the law of the LORD" (Ps 1:1a, 2a).

The world is full of contradictory voices. Opinions abound about diets, politics, morality, entertainment, and more, with each voice clamoring for our attention. Finding good counsel in the noise can feel overwhelming.

Turning away from sin requires us to sift through all the stuff of our lives, sorting out what leads us closer to God and what leads us away. The transformation we seek in Lent involves finding the voices that echo God's word in the distracting din. The most important voice we can invite to guide us is that of the Holy Spirit.

Holy Spirit—Advocate and Counselor—show me the heart of the Father.

Sit in silence with the Lord.

Think of a person who helps you draw closer to God. Offer a prayer of thanksgiving for them.

† **"Blessed the one who follows not the counsel of the wicked . . . But delights in the law of the LORD." Come Holy Spirit, help me hear God's voice, so I may draw closer to Christ. Amen.**

Friday after Ash Wednesday

† Create in me a clean heart, O God.

"My sacrifice, O God, is a contrite spirit; a heart contrite and humbled, O God, you will not spurn" (Ps 51:19).

Contemporary American culture prizes individual achievements and productivity as the pinnacle of life. It convinces us to credit success to our own merits, categorizing failure as moral inferiority. These attitudes can creep into our faith lives, making us like the self-righteous Pharisee who looks down on the tax collector in Jesus's parable (see Luke 18:9–14). We presume we are righteous because of what we have done, rather than humbling ourselves before our merciful God.

In reality, everything we have is a gift from God, even our very breath. We have nothing to offer the Lord that God does not already have. All we can offer is a heart open to God's love and to withhold nothing from God's tender care.

Lord Jesus, Son of God, I place my life into your hands.

Sit in silence with the Lord.

What are you holding back from God? Ask for the grace to offer it fully to the Lord.

† "My sacrifice, O God, is a contrite spirit; a heart contrite and humbled, O God, you will not spurn." Take my heart, Lord Jesus. It is all I have. I give it freely. Make my heart your own. Amen.

Saturday after Ash Wednesday

† Create in me a clean heart, O God.

"Hearken, O LORD, to my prayer and attend to the
sound of my pleading" (Ps 86:6).

Pain and grief are unavoidable parts of life. Scripture shows us
that, in these circumstances, sometimes the only way we humans
can approach God is through pleading. Imploring God to act
expresses how deeply we desire something different. There is no
shame in pleading. It humbles us and helps us remember how
very much we need God.

What we also see in scripture is a God who is moved by our
pleading and who cares about the things we care about. God may
not always respond with the outcome we hope for, but God is
always close to us, even when we do not sense it. Do not hesitate
to call on the Lord.

O God, hear the cries of my heart and be close to me.

Sit in silence with the Lord.

Choose an intention close to your heart and spend a few moments
pleading with God to act.

**† "Hearken, O LORD, to my prayer and attend to the sound of my
pleading." God, I need you. I will always need you. Turn your ear to
me and hear my cries. Draw close to me. Amen.**

Sunday, First Week of Lent

† Renew me, Lord, and revive my soul.

"Say to the LORD, 'My refuge and fortress,
my God in whom I trust'" (Ps 91:2).

For most of human history, living near a fortress (within its shadow) meant better security. Its walls were protection and refuge from attacking forces. It was where one would flee in great need and find safety as a last defense.

Though we may not need a physical fortress, we all need a place of refuge in our spiritual lives. We need somewhere to fly when the things that oppress our spirits, attack our well-being, or tempt us into despair come calling. In those times, fly unto God's protection. Let God be the refuge for the weary soul.

Lord, my God, help me seek shelter in you.

Sit in silence with the Lord.

Think of a moment when you needed God as a refuge. Recall and ponder what feelings and insights you had.

† "Say to the LORD, 'My refuge and fortress, my God in whom I trust'" (Ps 91:2). Lord, be my refuge when I have nowhere else to turn. I trust in you. Amen.

Monday, First Week of Lent

† Renew me, Lord, and revive my soul.

"The law of the LORD is perfect, refreshing the soul" (Ps 19:8a).

The law of the Lord is perfect and refreshes our souls because that law helps us better understand the world around us and the God who made it and loved us into being. As parents know well, established rules, clear boundaries, and reasonable expectations are essential for healthy human development. They provide structure which helps us navigate daily life—from mundane tasks to growing healthy, loving relationships. We thrive when we understand how things are ordered.

Embracing the law of the Lord enables us to understand God more fully. By knowing what God considers good and evil, we can better comprehend what God wants *for* and *of* us. Our Lenten disciplines of prayer, fasting, and almsgiving allow us to refine our habits and realign our priorities with the beauty and truth of the way of God—the truth that our destiny is determined not by the worst of our behaviors but rather by the gracious and merciful love of God, who would rather die than live without us.

The law of the Lord is indeed perfect; it cleanses and renews my soul!

Sit in silence with the Lord.

Ask God for help realigning your life in an area that you feel is out of sync with what God wants from and for you.

† "The law of the LORD is perfect, refreshing the soul." Lord, help me know the peace of obeying your will. Amen.

Tuesday, First Week of Lent

† Renew me, Lord, and revive my soul.

"The LORD is close to the brokenhearted; and those who are crushed in spirit he saves" (Ps 34:19).

Our world is full of brokenhearted people who are crushed in spirit. Oftentimes we find ourselves with broken hearts and crushed spirits of our own, in distress at events in our own lives or the suffering we see all around us. If the Lord is close to the brokenhearted, if God saves those whose spirits are crushed, where might we find that divine presence in our pain?

The answer lies, for Christians, in the crucified Christ. Jesus's body broken; Jesus's heart pierced; Jesus's anguished cry in the loneliness and horror of death. In Jesus Christ, God draws near to the broken, bruised, and forgotten. In Jesus Christ, God hears our cries and offers salvation to us who are, at times, crushed in spirit. Redeeming us means knowing fully what our suffering is by sharing in it. Love cannot be expressed without nearness. Jesus saves us in the midst of our suffering because he loves us. There is nothing that is too far from God's love to be redeemed.

Jesus, suffering savior, redeem my heart.

Sit in silence with the Lord.

Tell the Lord about something that causes you distress. Ask Jesus to share your pain.

† Lord Jesus, draw me close to you. Whatever is broken in my life, let it be made whole. "The LORD is close to the brokenhearted; and those who are crushed in spirit he saves." Amen.

Wednesday, First Week of Lent

† Renew me, Lord, and revive my soul.

"A clean heart create for me, O God, and a steadfast spirit renew within me" (Ps 51:12).

Only God can create a clean heart within us. Only God is able to steady our hearts so that we can follow in the Lord's ways. Despite our best intentions, our human will is not always enough to overcome temptation and sin. We are not always unwavering in our commitment to God's covenant, nor do our actions always follow the teachings of Jesus. We need the grace and mercy of God to continually renew our spirits and restore us to friendship with our Triune God. We must seek forgiveness in humility and honesty, knowing that we have fallen short of who we desire to be.

Forgiveness does not only restore us to a state of grace; it renews our spirits and helps us grow as disciples of Christ. Forgiveness brings comfort and relief, joy and hope. It is a medicine, and it reinvigorates the soul. In forgiveness, we see the truth and depth of God's love for us and we see our truest selves.

Lord, in your mercy, purify my heart.

Sit in silence with the Lord.

When have you experienced forgiveness—from God, another person, or yourself? Tell the Lord what that experience meant to you.

† Lord God, renew my spirit and make of me a witness to your steadfast and eternal love. "A clean heart create for me, O God, and a steadfast spirit renew within me." Amen.

Thursday, First Week of Lent

† Renew me, Lord, and revive my soul.

"The LORD will complete what he has done for me; your kindness, O
LORD, endures forever" (Ps 138:8).

The Lord will complete what he has done for us. As Christians
who believe Jesus has risen from the dead, we know that God
has won the victory for all time and that God makes good on his
promises. This is why we can exclaim that the Lord's kindness
endures forever: because Jesus died and is risen and no powers,
no sin, no evil—not even death—can triumph against the saving
power of God.

So, when we find ourselves weary from life and its struggles,
when we find ourselves burdened and broken down by the injus-
tices and evils we see around us, we should not give in to despair.
God has already begun the work of restoring all of creation. God
has already made a way out of no way. God has already begun
refining us for the glory of his holy name. God will complete what
he has begun for us. Let us live in a manner that affirms our belief
and proclaims to everyone that the Lord's kindness endures forever. O God, complete what you have begun in me.

Sit in silence with the Lord.

Take a few moments to reflect on your story, thinking about how
Jesus has impacted your life. Try sharing a short version of your
transformation with a trusted friend or family member this week.
Watch for further insight.

**† God, I know you will complete what you have begun for me. Help
me to show my hope and trust in you. "The LORD will complete
what he has done for me; your kindness, O LORD, endures forever."
Amen.**

Friday, First Week of Lent

† Renew me, Lord, and revive my soul.

"If you, O LORD, mark iniquities, LORD, who can stand? But with you is forgiveness, that you may be revered" (Ps 130:3–4).

God is perfect. And if God were to mark our iniquities, to keep a tally of our sins compared to divine perfection, no one could stand in the divine presence. The holiest of saints could not measure up. Even our Blessed Mother was immaculately conceived in order to be freed from original sin.

But with the Lord there is forgiveness. With the Lord there is freedom from sin. Through Jesus we are clothed with divine life and can stand in God's presence as beloved daughters and sons, co-heirs with Christ himself. God's mercy shows perfection more than judgment because it demonstrates God's kindness and compassion. God does not use power to demean and humiliate. God's perfect power is love, which raises up the lowly to eternal life.

Jesus, in your mercy, raise me up to new life.

Sit in silence with the Lord.

Think of someone in your life who might need the hope that comes with God's mercy. Pray for them to experience the joy of forgiveness.

† Thank you, Lord, for counting me worthy to stand in your presence. May I always honor all you have done for me. "If you, O LORD, mark iniquities, LORD, who can stand? But with you is forgiveness, that you may be revered." Amen.

Saturday, First Week of Lent

† Renew me, Lord, and revive my soul.

"You have commanded that your precepts be diligently kept. Oh, that I might be firm in the ways of keeping your statutes!" (Ps 119:4–5).

All throughout scripture God is exhorting people to keep the commandments. Jesus tells us that not one letter of the Law will pass away. To be a follower of Christ means to try diligently to keep God's commands.

Human as we are, we will not be perfect in following God's law. There may be times when, like the psalmist, we cry out to God, "Oh, that I might be firm in the ways of keeping your statutes." God knows we need help and will hear our cries. The Holy Spirit will always come when we ask.

The key, though, is that we must be humble enough to ask for the Spirit's assistance. At the heart of the commandments is the acknowledgment that God is God and we are not. Keeping the commandments diligently requires us to relinquish our pride and trust the God who loves us. God takes joy in our efforts and will not fail to come to our aid.

Holy Spirit, come, and help me live the Father's commands.

Sit in silence with the Lord.

Look back at the past week and the moments you have tried to be faithful to God's commands. Ask Jesus to help you see those moments through his eyes.

† Jesus, I want to keep your commandments. Send down your Spirit so I may be firm in following your will. "You have commanded that your precepts be diligently kept. Oh, that I might be firm in the ways of keeping your statutes!" Amen.

Sunday, Second Week of Lent

† Deliver me, Lord, from death into life.

"Of you my heart speaks; you my glance seeks" (Ps 27:8).

Our hearts are made for God. In their deepest depths our hearts speak to us of the Lord, longing to find the Divine Presence who created us. Like a lover enraptured by their beloved, our soul's glance is seeking out the One who can complete us. That yearning for the Lord reveals itself in all facets of human life, from the highest art forms to the ways we chase pleasure that can never fulfill.

In this Lenten season we have a chance to ask ourselves what we do to address that longing deep within. Do we embrace it and find ways to connect with the Lord? Do we avoid it because it requires facing our own mortality and frailty? Do we leave it for another day when we are older, or have more time, or fewer demands in our lives? Lent gives us the opportunity to turn toward God. How might we capitalize on this season and listen to what our hearts are yearning to say?

Lord Jesus, let me see your face.

Sit in silence with the Lord.

At the end of the day, take a few minutes to review the events of the day. Ask the Spirit to show you where you were seeking the Lord and where you were not.

† Lord, my heart speaks of you and my glance seeks you. Let me rest in your presence forever. "Of you my heart speaks; you my glance seeks." Amen.

Monday, Second Week of Lent

† Deliver me, Lord, from death into life.

"Let the prisoners' sighing come before you; with your great power free those doomed to death" (Ps 79:11).

There were many moments in childhood when I was caught in wrongdoing. There was nothing quite as anxiety-inducing as the sinking weight of knowing I had to face the consequences of my choices. I knew I deserved whatever penalty might come, and I still dreaded facing my parents. And in so many of those moments I would beg my parents to be lenient and forgive me for the bad thing I had done.

This psalm draws us into a similar position before Our Lord. Knowing our sins, we come sighing in repentance, begging for God's great power to free us. We know that we do not deserve grace, and yet we ask anyway. We ask because, thanks to Jesus, we can approach the throne of grace with confidence (Heb 4:16). God took the consequence of our sins, and our sentence has been commuted. What marvelous grace we've been given to have sighs turned to shouts of joy!

I thank you, Lord, that you have set me free.

Sit in silence with the Lord.

Take a few minutes to reflect on the joy of salvation. Revel in God's goodness and mercy.

† Jesus, thank you for freeing me from death. I do not deserve your love, but I am grateful. "Let the prisoners' sighing come before you; with your great power free those doomed to death." Amen.

Tuesday, Second Week of Lent

† Deliver me, Lord, from death into life.

"Why do you recite my statutes, and profess my covenant with your
mouth, Though you hate discipline and cast my words behind you?"
(Ps 50:16bc–17).

How often do we recite prayers and profess our faith in public, and
then go on to deny it by the way we live daily? Even though we
know God's statutes, could someone else tell that we *live* them? Are
God's words leading us forward? Or have we cast them behind us?

Every Christian must answer these questions. These questions challenge us to acknowledge our own hypocrisy, turn back
to God, and recommit to following Jesus. We are not perfect. We
are human. And we will sin. Will we respond to God's invitation
to restore our relationship with him, or will we compound our
errors by pretending we don't need God's forgiveness?

For that is the true hypocrisy: believing we can do anything
apart from God's grace and mercy and that we don't need heal-
ing. God does not expect perfection. We have the sacrAmen.ts as
testAmen.t to that. God asks for faithfulness. Will we only profess
God's covenant with our mouths, or will we remain faithful to it
in humility and hope?

Jesus, help me live what I believe.

Sit in silence with the Lord.

Ask the Holy Spirit to show you one way you could better reflect
Jesus to the people in your life today.

**† God, help me to practice what I preach so that others may see
your goodness and believe in you. "Why do you recite my statutes,
and profess my covenant with your mouth, Though you hate discipline and cast my words behind you?" Amen.**

Wednesday, Second Week of Lent

† Deliver me, Lord, from death into life.

"You will free me from the snare they set for me,
for you are my refuge" (Ps 31:5).

Evil is greedy. It camouflages itself as good to make us fall prey to its illusions. Snares like vice, addiction, ignorance, injustice, and apathy can trap us in cycles of sin, turning people into objects to be used until spent. Evil has no concern for our individuality and promise. The world, too, can be indifferent to sin's captives. The worst impulses of our culture are overlooked as children of God become caricatures of God's image dwelling within them. Culture simply moves forward, unconcerned about those left behind.

The world may be indifferent to us, but God is *passionately for us*. God does not want us to be harmed by evil. God wants us to triumph over it. God is the refuge from the many ways that evil attempts to cage us and—through Jesus—sets a path by which we can safely navigate the hazards. Let's remember to trust in the Lord, our refuge and our strength!

Father, keep me safe from evil's snare.

Sit in silence with the Lord.

What snares do you see on your path currently? Ask God to help you navigate them safely.

† Jesus, I trust that you will be my refuge. Guide me safely on the path of life. "You will free me from the snare they set for me, for you are my refuge." Amen.

Thursday, Second Week of Lent

"For the LORD watches over the way of the just, but the way of the wicked vanishes" (Ps 1:6).

The way of the wicked vanishes because the world's promises are empty. The world values things like youth, beauty, and health, which are all temporary in this life. The awards and accolades we win today will be given to a new recipient the following year. Money, houses, cars, vacations, and even career success cannot fill our most profound desires. Ultimately, only God's way will truly fulfill us. Only what comes from God lasts forever.

God is eternal and cannot vanish or change. God always was, God is now, and God always will be. God's promises are not fleeting or misleading. God's promises, from the Creation of the world to the life, death, and Resurrection of Jesus Christ, are always fulfilled. They are yes and Amen. for every age that was and is to come.

God calls us to eternal life and watches over us whenever we try to walk in his ways. God gives us the Word, the sacrAmen.ts, and the Church so we do not have to walk alone. When we seek God's face, the Lord blesses our efforts. Let's seek him with all our hearts.

Keep me in the way of the just, O Lord.

Sit in silence with the Lord.

Think about a promise God has fulfilled. How can you show appreciation for that today?

† **Lord, watch over me today. Guide my feet to walk in your way, so I might have eternal life. "For the LORD watches over the way of the just, but the way of the wicked vanishes." Amen.**

Friday, Second Week of Lent

† Deliver me, Lord, from death into life.

"Remember the marvels the Lord has done" (Ps 105:5a).

God's love does marvelous deeds. The love of God created the heavens and the earth. The love of God called Abraham, Isaac, and Jacob, forming a new people living in covenant with the Most High. God's love freed the Israelites from slavery in Egypt, brought them into the promised land, established a kingdom, sent them prophets, and brought them home from exile. And God's love became incarnate in Jesus of Nazareth to overturn sin and death forever.

In Baptism, we became part of this life-changing story. All the marvels God has done for Israel, all the wonders seen at the hands of Jesus, were done for us. God's miracles, signs, and wonders were done so we could know God and so no barriers could exist between us. The story of how we came to know and love Jesus may not be dramatic. The ways the Lord has transformed our hearts over the years might be incremental. But they are additional chapters in the tale of God's marvelous works. Remember the marvels the Lord has done—for his people, and most especially for you.

Thank you, Lord, for the great wonders you have done.

Sit in silence with the Lord.

Sometime today, tell someone you trust about a good thing God has done for you.

**† God, you have done truly marvelous deeds for me.
You are worthy to be praised! "Remember the marvels
the Lord has done." Amen.**

Saturday, Second Week of Lent

† **Deliver me, Lord, from death into life.**

"As far as the east is from the west, so far has he put our transgressions from us" (Ps 103:11–12).

Through Jesus, God has put our transgressions as far away from us as the east is from the west—so far away from us that it would be impossible to find them again. Because of Jesus's death and Resurrection, God will forgive us *anything* when we repent.

Do we really believe that? Many of us become mired in guilt, dwelling on our inadequacies and replaying our worst actions over and over again in our heads. We latch onto our sin, hold it close to us, refusing to forgive ourselves when God would forget it all. We do this to other people, too. We hold on to their minor misdeeds long after they apologize, mature, or try to make Amen. ds. We forget that Jesus commands us to love our enemies, pray for those who persecute us, and forgive seventy times seven times. In short, we sometimes give sin more power than we allow God.

But God's power is greater than sin. We can give up guilt, shame, and grievances. They can be put as far from us as east from west. All we need to do is give them to the Lord.

God, let me never give power to any but you.

Sit in silence with the Lord.

Ask God to show you something you need to let go and pray for Jesus to put it far away from you.

† **Thank you, Jesus, for putting my transgressions far away from me. You are my hope and my salvation! "As far as the east is from the west, so far has he put our transgressions from us." Amen.**

Sunday, Third Week of Lent

† Shepherd me, O Lord, in the truth of your word.

"For as the heavens are high above the earth, so surpassing is his kindness toward those who fear him" (Ps 103:11).

It is hard to fathom how good and kind God is. We can only hint at it with words such as the psalmist uses here in Psalm 103. Because how could we describe the goodness of God in a way that would sum up all he has done? What words could we find to express the wellspring of joy at God's marvelous deeds throughout history? How about just the things Jesus has done in our own lives? There is a reason that the last line of John's gospel states, "But there are also many other things that Jesus did; if every one of them were written down, I suppose that the world itself could not contain the books that would be written" (Jn 21:25, *New Revised Standard Version, Catholic Edition*).

While we cannot fathom God's kindness, we can imitate it. God's love is love that gives of self, not counting the cost. It is a love that seeks out the broken, weary, sin-sick, oppressed, and overlooked. God's is a love that offers care and compassion when the world has none. It is not too much to pay attention to those we encounter to find ways to choose their good over our own. We can find the places where God needs hands to heal and help and where we might offer our own. God's kindness may be hard to fathom, but we can help others experience it if we're willing.

Sit in silence with the Lord.

Imitate God's kindness with a small act of service for another person today.

† Lord, help me to be kind like you, so others may know your goodness. "For as the heavens are high above the earth, so surpassing is his kindness toward those who fear him." Amen.

Monday, Third Week of Lent

† **Shepherd me, O Lord, in the truth of your word.**

"Athirst is my soul for God, the living God. When shall I go and behold the face of God?" (Ps 42:3).

Thirst can be all-consuming. Thirst awakens our survival instincts and grabs hold of our attention until it is quenched. It drives us to seek a source of water, which becomes a source of life. A soul thirsting for God is searching for its most fundAmen.tal need. Like living water, the Living God is the soul's most life-giving source. A soul thirsting for God longs to go and behold the face of God because nothing else will satisfy.

Perhaps you remember a time when your soul felt dry and empty. Perhaps you are in a spiritual desert right now. Or maybe entering into the wilderness of Lent has reminded you of how desperate you are to see God's face. Wherever you find yourself, Jesus is crying out to you. "Let anyone who is thirsty come to me," he says, "and let the one who believes in me drink" (Jn 7:37b–38a, NRSVCE). Jesus wants to refresh your soul each and every day with his love. Draw near to him to be revived and renewed. Let his love be a waterfall of grace for you. Trust in Jesus. In him you will find the face of God.

Lord Jesus, quench my soul's thirst with your grace.

Sit in silence with the Lord.

Doodle or write a few words to describe how Jesus refreshes you.

† **Jesus, you are Living Water. Show me your face. Refresh and renew my soul today and always. "Athirst is my soul for God, the living God. When shall I go and behold the face of God?" Amen.**

Tuesday, Third Week of Lent

† **Shepherd me, O Lord, in the truth of your word.**

"Your ways, O LORD, make known to me; teach
me your paths, Guide me in your truth and teach me,
for you are God my savior" (Ps 24:4–5ab).

Walking in truth means walking in relationship with God. The psalmist does not recite various statutes and practices for growing in holiness but rather asks the Lord to teach and guide, to lead the way so that we can follow. God's ways are relational and invite us into communion. Knowing God's ways means knowing God.

This becomes even clearer when we reflect on the work of the Triune God. The Father entered into covenants with Israel, giving the Law and the prophets to act as guides. The Son became a human being, died, and rose in order to teach us the paths to the Father. The Spirit descended to guide us toward what is true and keep us away from the lies that would separate us from God's love.

How might we grow in our relationship with the Triune God today? Where can we be drawn into deeper communion with the Father, Son, and Holy Spirit? How might we invite the Divine Trinity to guide us and teach us truth?

O God—Father, Son, and Holy Spirit—teach me to know you and to know your ways.

Sit in silence with the Lord.

Think of a moment when you saw the Trinity working in your life. Thank God for the gift of divine guidance.

† **God, help me to know you better so I may always walk in your ways. "Your ways, O LORD, make known to me; teach me your paths, Guide me in your truth and teach me, for you are God my savior." Amen.**

Wednesday, Third Week of Lent

† **Shepherd me, O Lord, in the truth of your word.**

"He sends forth his command to the earth;
swiftly runs his word!" (Ps 147:15).

When God sends forth a command—when God speaks the Word—things happen. In Genesis, God speaks and all creation comes into being. Jesus commands people to be healed, the sea to quiet, and the dead to rise. God's Word is effective and powerful. Where it is heard and received, it transforms everything.

God's Word also runs swiftly. Unlike a king of old who must depend on the swiftness of horses or humans running messages, God's Word is brought by the Holy Spirit, the most reliable messenger. The Spirit speaks directly to our hearts in the ways we can best understand the Lord. As long as we are open to the Spirit's promptings, there is no barrier between hearing God's Word and receiving it.

The question for each of us is whether we will receive and be transformed by God's Word when we hear it. Will we spend time reading it and listening to the Spirit's promptings? Will we be shaped and formed by it each day so that we are transformed to be more like God? And more pointedly, will we, too, become messengers for the Lord so others may also be transformed?

Father, speak your Word into my life.

Sit in silence with the Lord.

Place a favorite Bible verse in a place you will see it every day. Recite it when you need a moment to pause.

† **Lord, I praise you for the goodness of your Word. May it take root in me and bear great fruit. "He sends forth his command to the earth; swiftly runs his word!" Amen.**

Thursday, Third Week of Lent

† Shepherd me, O Lord, in the truth of your word.

"For he is our God, and we are the people he shepherds, the flock he guides" (Ps 95:7).

I'm not very good at letting Christ shepherd me. If Jesus is the Good Shepherd, then I am the lamb whom he frees from being stuck in a fence only to get stuck right back in that barrier once again. I resist the Lord's guidance. I run away from the flock and from his protection. I am an obstinate sheep who thinks I can make it on my own without the shepherd's rod and staff.

Lent is a time when I remember Christ's faithful guidance. It allows me to create space to listen for the Shepherd's voice calling me back to his flock when I wander off. Jesus wants me to be part of his people, the covenant community sealed by his sacrifice on the Cross. This Lent, I rejoice in the truth that the God of Israel has always been faithful to me and that I can never wander so far that Jesus Christ won't come looking for me.

Shepherd me, Lord Jesus, and help me to be guided by your love.

Sit in silence with the Lord.

Reflect on your Lenten practice thus far. Share with God what has been fruitful and what has been challenging.

† Jesus, you are the Good Shepherd. Let me never stray from your love. "For he is our God, and we are the people he shepherds, the flock he guides." Amen.

Friday, Third Week of Lent

† Shepherd me, O Lord, in the truth of your word.

"There shall be no strange god among you nor shall you worship any alien god" (Ps 81:10).

It's deceptively easy to make something into a strange and alien god. To worship something is to give it reverence, adoration, and honor. Worship engages our whole person and devotes our energy to that thing above all else. We honor and devote our energy to many good things—family, work, rest, justice, health, peace, recreation. If we do not keep these in proper perspective, we can easily slip into giving hours upon hours to them before ever considering God. We likely never intentionally reject God, but we let ourselves slowly turn our attention to another good thing, until we can no longer see the Lord. In our culture, idols are not carved to other deities. They are made by focusing on good *things* rather than Goodness itself.

God reminds us again and again in the scriptures that true worship is living out God's word in our lives each day. To worship God, we must give our full devotion, reverence, and energy to the Lord in every circumstance of our day. Our energy, time, and honor can still be given over to good things, as long as, in all that is good, we focus on God and seek to give him honor through it.

Lord, help me to keep my focus on you, so I can honor you in all that I do.

Sit in silence with the Lord.

Ask the Holy Spirit to help you see where in your life you need to honor God more fully. Commit to a simple action to take today which will help change it.

† God, help me to always put you first. I love you with all my heart. "There shall be no strange god among you nor shall you worship any alien god." Amen.

Saturday, Third Week of Lent

† Shepherd me, O Lord, in the truth of your word.

"Be bountiful, O Lord, to Zion in your kindness by rebuilding the walls of Jerusalem" (Ps 51:20).

When the Jewish people were in exile in Babylon, it's easy to imagine the people praying fervently, "Be bountiful, O Lord, to Zion in your kindness by rebuilding the walls of Jerusalem." Scripture shows us how unflinchingly people like Daniel clung to their hope that they would return to the land of Judah and rebuild the Temple of the Lord. The words of Psalm 51 must have spoken to their yearning as well as to their trust in God. They clung to God's promises and to the burning hope that God would make good. What a sublime day it must have been when they could go back again!

As Christians, the message of Jesus is our great hope. In his words and ways, we find hope that things can be different in this life, that the kingdom can and will break out among us. In his death and Resurrection, we find hope for eternal life, hope that evil does not have the final say because Christ is victorious. While we live in exile now, we can ask the Lord to be bountiful to us in his kindness, because we know that someday we will return to the heavenly Jerusalem to be with our God forever.

Lord Jesus, renew my hope and let me see your kindness.

Sit in silence with the Lord.

Where do you find hope in the message of Jesus? Thank him for these things today.

† God, show us your kindness, so that we may show the world the joy of your salvation. "Be bountiful, O Lord, to Zion in your kindness by rebuilding the walls of Jerusalem." Amen.

Sunday, Fourth Week of Lent

† The Lord turns every sorrow into joy.

"Glorify the LORD with me, let us together extol his name" (Ps 34:4).

Glorify the Lord with me this Sunday. Let us together extol his name as we gather around the altar. Let us praise and honor Jesus for the miracles he has worked, the paths he has made straight before us, and the redemption he has won for us. It is his great name by which we are transformed and his great name that we proclaim at every Mass. Every Sunday we have the privilege to gather with other followers of Jesus and tell the stories of all he has done. We get to say to each other, "Look how good the Lord has been to us!" And, most remarkably of all, we get to receive the Lord himself in the Eucharist.

This Sunday, let's try to move beyond rote responses at Mass and give our whole selves to praise. Let every story of God's grace working in our lives fill our hearts and come out in our voices. Glorify the Lord with words and songs and silence. Join with the angels and saints in the eternal hymn of praise. In one voice, with all creation, together let us extol his name!

Lord, I praise your name for you have been so good to me!

Sit in silence with the Lord.

If you feel comfortable, proclaim the names and deeds of God aloud as an act of praise. Or recite the *Gloria* from Sunday Mass as an act of praise.

† Lord God, I praise you for all you are and all you have done! "Glorify the LORD with me, let us together extol his name." Amen.

Monday, Fourth Week of Lent

† The Lord turns every sorrow into joy.

"You changed my mourning into dancing; O LORD, my God, forever will I give you thanks" (Ps 30:12a, 13b).

You've changed our mourning to dancing, Lord, and we will give you thanks forever. You have taken the things that have broken our hearts and caused us to despair, and the sins that make us blush with shame, and turned them into moments of resilience, hope, freedom, and new life through the Precious Blood of Jesus. We can dance and shout because, in remembering the grief and pain, we now see the victory and transformation you have wrought in our lives.

There will be more grief, sorrow, and pain to come. Human life will always have its hardships and losses. Death will take loved ones and our bodies will become weak and frail. People will hurt us and we will hurt others. Our minds and souls will grapple with emotions and realities beyond our ability to understand. The bitter will always mingle with the sweet.

Even though the hurt might still be there, we know your Holy Spirit will be the balm for all our wounds. You endured the Cross for us, and we know you will never abandon or forsake us. Lord, we trust you to change our mourning into dancing once again.

Sit in silence with the Lord.

Tell the Lord about your grief and fears. Ask God to transform them into glory.

† Lord, help me to see joy in the midst of grief and hope amid my fears. "You changed my mourning into dancing; O LORD, my God, forever will I give you thanks." Amen.

Tuesday, Fourth Week of Lent

† The Lord turns every sorrow into joy.

"God is our refuge and our strength, an ever-present help in distress. Therefore, we fear not, though the earth be shaken and mountains plunge into the depths of the sea" (Ps 46:2–3).

If the earth was shaken and mountains began to plunge into the depths of the sea, it would be hard to remain calm. Something so jarring would be petrifying. We might even believe we were seeing the end of the world. Terror is a natural response to catastrophe. That's what makes the psalmist's statement so profound. To announce that "God is our refuge and our strength, an ever-present help in distress; therefore we fear not" is an act of complete trust in God. It is a proclamation that nothing is more powerful than God and that we walk in freedom from fear because we know God is with us.

In a world where there are evils and trauma just as damaging to our spirits as any natural disaster, to have this kind of faith is revolutionary. To walk in freedom from fear is extraordinary when we are coping with mental or physical illness, broken relationships, poverty, violence, and so many other ills. Will we let God be our refuge and strength when everything is falling apart?

Lord, give us faith to stand firm even though mountains plunge into the sea.

Sit in silence with the Lord.

Tell Jesus what is holding you back from trusting him. Ask him to show you how to grow in trust.

† Lord, be my ever-present help. Give me faith to walk in your freedom. "God is our refuge and our strength, an ever-present help in distress. Therefore, we fear not, though the earth be shaken and mountains plunge into the depths of the sea." Amen.

Wednesday, Fourth Week of Lent

† The Lord turns every sorrow into joy.

"The LORD lifts up all who are falling and raises up all who are bowed down" (Ps 145:14).

When we are bowed down and weary, God can raise us to new strength. When we are falling from the weight of sorrow, sin, or shame, God can lift us up into freedom and peace. Life is full of stresses and uncertainties, which can feel overwhelming as we simply try to make it through each day.

It's important to care for ourselves when we are weary. We cannot bear every burden or fight every battle without stopping to recover, and we certainly cannot do it by ourselves. Jesus himself is waiting to bear the burden with us if we only take a moment to pause. Let his invitation wash over you in this moment, and give yourself over to his gentle care. Hear his loving voice saying, "Come to me, all you that are weary and are carrying heavy burdens, and I will give you rest. Take my yoke upon you, and learn from me; for I am gentle and humble in heart, and you will find rest for your souls. For my yoke is easy, and my burden is light" (Mt 11:28–30, NRSVCE).

Loving God, I offer you my burdens and give myself into your gentle care.

Sit in silence with the Lord.

Allow yourself a moment without action. Silently rest in the presence of the Holy Spirit.

† Lift me up, Lord, so I may find new strength in you.
"The LORD lifts up all who are falling and raises up all who are bowed down." Amen.

Thursday, Fourth Week of Lent

† The Lord turns every sorrow into joy.

"Then he spoke of exterminating them, but Moses,
his chosen one, withstood him in the breach to
turn back his destructive wrath" (Ps 106:23).

I am in awe of the courage that Moses had. While he was receiving the Ten Commandments on Mount Sinai, the Israelites were worshiping a golden calf. In spite of his anger upon discovering their sin, Moses still went back to Sinai to ask God to spare the people. Like a lone warrior in battle, Moses stood in the breach between God's wrath and the people. He had the faith to approach God as a friend and ask for mercy, and God did relent from destroying all of Israel.

Moses's boldness gives me confidence to be daring in prayer. His assurance testifies to the power of intercessory prayer and its ability to transform the lives of others. It reminds me of the people who interceded for me at different stages of my life, to turn back the wrath of dark powers and principalities that seek to separate me from God. May we all have such powerful allies in our corner and be the same fierce champions for others.

Lord, give me the faith to be bold in prayer and to stand in the breach for others.

Sit in silence with the Lord.

Who has "stood in the breach" for you before God? Pray for that person today.

† Thank you for the people who have stood in the breach for me, Lord. "He spoke of exterminating them, but Moses, his chosen one, withstood him in the breach to turn back his destructive wrath." Amen.

Friday, Fourth Week of Lent

† The Lord turns every sorrow into joy.

"The LORD redeems the lives of his servants; no one incurs guilt who takes refuge in him" (Ps 34:23).

The Lord Jesus Christ redeems the lives of his servants through his Cross. He pays the price of our captivity to sin with his own life so we can be free from all the things that keep us bound. The worst things we have ever done to others—the addictions, the selfishness, the anger, the pettiness, the indifference—all of these are erased from the ledger when we turn to Christ. No one incurs guilt who takes refuge in him.

Will we allow Jesus to redeem the things we loathe about ourselves? Will we hand over the tally of our sins and accept liberation from our shackles? Can we resist the temptation to stay in chains because our hands and feet have become calloused from their chafing? How can we take refuge in him so guilt cannot hold sway over our lives any longer?

Let's begin today by acknowledging our sins and our need for rescue. Let's show our contrition and our resolve to start anew in a life free from slavery to sin. Let's take refuge in Our Lord and Savior Jesus Christ, who redeems the lives of his servants through his Cross.

Redeem me, Lord Jesus, as only you can do.

Sit in silence with the Lord.

Pray an act of contrition today or make up your own prayer asking God's forgiveness.

† God, I am sorry for my sins. Wipe away my guilt and redeem me. "The LORD redeems the lives of his servants; no one incurs guilt who takes refuge in him." Amen.

Saturday, Fourth Week of Lent

† The Lord turns every sorrow into joy.

"Let the malice of the wicked come to an end, but sustain the just, O searcher of heart and soul, O just God" (Ps 7:10).

"Let the malice of the wicked come to an end." This prayer could be uttered in any generation of human history. Evil has been with us since the beginning, a reality of the gift of free will. Just as we can choose good, we can also choose evil. Evil choices can impact the health and flourishing of others, as in the case of theft and abuse. Evil choices can also build on each other, creating forces like war, racism, and abject poverty. We often cannot feel anything but overwhelmed in the face of so much evil.

The second half of this prayer voices another truth we know deep in our bones—that God is just and does not tolerate evil. God is the searcher of heart and soul who will ultimately judge every heart. We beg God to sustain the just because we know that light is the only thing that can overcome darkness. We plead to end malice because we know only God can roll back the darkness and make justice flourish forever. This prayer may be echoed in every human generation, but God, who is faithful in every generation, can and will make it true.

Lord, roll back the darkness of evil so justice may flourish forever.

Sit in silence with the Lord.

Pray for an end to a particular evil, such as violence, racism, or hunger.

† Sustain all those who work for justice, O God. Let them see the fruits of their labors. "Let the malice of the wicked come to an end, but sustain the just, O searcher of heart and soul, O just God." Amen.

Sunday, Fifth Week of Lent

† Hear me, Lord, and despise not my prayer.

"Those that sow in tears shall reap rejoicing" (Ps 126:5).

The psalmist promised us that those who sow in tears shall reap rejoicing. Jesus proclaims in the Beatitudes, "Blessed are those who mourn, for they will be comforted" (Mt 5:4, NRSVCE), and in his ministry he heals the sick, raises the dead, and restores sinners to wholeness. Jesus's words and deeds are a foretaste of the kingdom, where tears sowed in sorrow are harvested as shouts of joy. There will be a day with no more tears, and Jesus's life, death, and Resurrection are proof positive that it's on its way.

Lent is also a foretaste of the kingdom of heaven. Our disciplines are the seeds planted to reap Easter joy. The work of the Holy Spirit cultivates the soil of our souls so growth and life will break forth. While we may not see miracles and wonders, we may just see transformed hearts. And our change is also evidence of what is to come—a day when sin and evil are rooted out and righteousness shall flower for all time. Let's use these final weeks of Lent to tend and till with patience and hope, as we look forward to the fruits of the Spirit's labor.

Come, Holy Spirit, and help me reap rejoicing.

Sit in silence with the Lord.

What has the Holy Spirit been cultivating in you during this Lenten season? Choose one action to engage in today to further that work.

† Holy Spirit, tend to my heart, so I may know Easter joy. "Those that sow in tears shall reap rejoicing." Amen.

April 7
Monday, Fifth Week of Lent

† Hear me, Lord, and despise not my prayer.

"Even though I walk in the dark valley I fear no evil; for you are at my side" (Ps 23:4ab).

Fear is a powerful motivator for action. Anticipating evil has caused reasonable people to act in ways we may have never thought possible. It can trick our minds and propel us to reject our most deeply held values. The dark valley of fear narrows our vision and keeps us from seeing the presence of God as well as the needs of others. Fear too often explains the worst of human behavior.

Disciples of Jesus need not fear evil, for God is by our side. When we worry that evil might befall us, we must recenter our whole selves on God's love and faithfulness. When fear narrows our vision, we need to remember that the Lord's rod and staff are guiding us through the dark valley. If we look for God's presence, we will find our way through. So, let's not let fear dictate our path. Instead, let's walk side by side with the Lord, whose perfect love casts out fear.

Lord Jesus, I trust your guidance, even in the darkest valley of fear.

Sit in silence with the Lord.

Reflect on the difference between your actions that are motivated by fear and those that are motivated by love. How can you operate from God's love instead of fear today?

† God, help me act from love and not fear. "Even though I walk in the dark valley I fear no evil; for you are at my side." Amen.

Tuesday, Fifth Week of Lent

† Hear me, Lord, and despise not my prayer.

"He has regarded the prayer of the destitute, and not despised their prayer" (Ps 102:18).

God regards the prayer of the destitute and does not count our lowliness against us. We do not need to be powerful, rich, beautiful, or healthy to be heard. God does not make us prove our worthiness in order to draw close to him, nor does he despise our prayers when the world would count us out. God's blessing, favor, and mercy are poured out to the meek and poor without counting the cost. The generous love of the Father hears and cherishes every prayer we offer.

God urges us to let go of whatever it is we believe we have to be in order to be loved by him. There is nothing we can do to earn more of God's love and no reason we ever need to. God would pay any price for us, and in fact Jesus did so in order that nothing might keep us from understanding that we are beloved and we are enough. The only response we need to make to that love is to accept it and love God wholeheartedly in return.

God, help me accept your lavish and unending love.

Sit in silence with the Lord.

Make a list of things you think God loves about you and for a few minutes just bask in the glow of divine love.

† Thank you, Lord, for loving and hearing me. "He has regarded the prayer of the destitute, and not despised their prayer." Amen.

Wednesday, Fifth Week of Lent

† **Hear me, Lord, and despise not my prayer.**

"The LORD swore an oath to David in truth, he will
never turn back from it: 'Your own offspring, I will set upon your
throne'" (Ps 132:11).

The Lord swore an oath to David that David's offspring would be
set upon the throne of Israel and that his line would not fail. In
spite of the failures of individual kings and of the people of Judah,
God remained faithful in his promises. Jesus fulfilled God's covenant with David, freeing his people from their sins and establish-
ing a reign that will never fail. Jesus now lives forever in heaven
with his very human body that will never decay or perish. He
is living and active in our lives even when we cannot see him
face-to-face.

What great news this is for us! In Jesus we see God make good
on a promise and receive a new promise of what's in store for us.
One day we will share in Jesus's Resurrection in the new heavens
and the new earth, with bodies that will be restored to life forever.
And because God has fulfilled one covenant, we also know that
God will never turn back from an oath. What a glorious hope to
hold in our hearts this Lent!

Thank you, Lord, for the hope of the resurrection.

Sit in silence with the Lord.

Think of people who have followed through on their promises for
you. Offer a prayer for them today.

† **God, your promises are true. May I trust you will always make
good. "The LORD swore an oath to David in truth, he will never
turn back from it: 'Your own offspring, I will set upon your
throne.'" Amen.**

Thursday, Fifth Week of Lent

† Hear me, Lord, and despise not my prayer.

"Look to the LORD in his strength; seek to
serve him constantly" (Ps 105:4).

Look to the Lord in his strength. God's strength is found in love, mercy, compassion, kindness, and giving to others without setting conditions. Take strength from God's strength and goodness from God's goodness. Let God's word become imbued in every part of your life. Let it flow from your lips and be written in your every action. Look to the Lord to see how you should be.

Seek, also, to serve God constantly. Be on the lookout for ways to do good in imitation of Christ's humility. Be ready to do what is good when it is convenient and when it is not, when it is expected and when it is not, and when it is encouraged and when it is not. We should be attentive to what is happening around us and prepared to respond to God's promptings within our hearts. In this way we will not only be serving the Lord but also be able to share some of God's strength with others. Look to the Lord in his strength and seek to serve him constantly.

God, help me to imitate the strength of your love.

Sit in silence with the Lord.

Looking at the day ahead, where might you find an opportunity to do good for another person? Come up with a way to do it without any recognition.

† Lord give me your strength to seek you and serve you always.
"Look to the LORD in his strength; seek to serve him constantly."
Amen.

Friday, Fifth Week of Lent

† Hear me, Lord, and despise not my prayer.

"In my distress I called upon the LORD and
cried out to my God" (Ps 18:7a).

In times of distress, I have called upon the Lord and cried out to my God. Those were times when I had no stores of resilience left and the emotional pain was too great for me to bear. The mask of competence and control I put on for the world was stripped away. All that was left was my raw and ragged soul, bared fully before the Lord. In those moments, the only recourse I had left was to cry out to God and hope that God would hear me.

I know that God hears the prayers of our distress. I know because Jesus himself sighed and cried, "Ephphatha" (Be opened) (Mk 7:34). He wept and cried, "Lazarus, come out!" (Jn 11:43). And from the Cross he cried, "Eli, Eli, lema sabachthani?" (My God, my God, why have you forsaken me?) (Mt 27:46), and the earth shook. More intimately, I know that God hears our cries because Christ heard mine and he bore pain with me. We have a God who suffered like us and who will sit in suffering with us. Do not hesitate to cry out to him whenever you're in need.

Lord, give me the courage to cry out to you in my need.

Sit in silence with the Lord.

Recall a time when God comforted you in distress. Thank God for the gifts that came from his presence.

† O God, I know you hear me when I cry. Let me never forget that you are with me. "In my distress I called upon the LORD and cried out to my God." Amen.

Saturday, Fifth Week of Lent

† Hear me, Lord, and despise not my prayer.

"The LORD knows the plans of man; they are
like a fleeting breath" (Ps 94:11).

To the Lord, our plans are like a fleeting breath. We draw up schema and design systems. Many of them are focused on momentary honors or rewards that don't last beyond a few years. But even the best things we do as humans, the things that last centuries, are gone in an instant in the face of eternity. Our plans are nothing compared to God's eternal design.

God's plans, however, are everlasting. Our wildest dreams are too small for God. God knows our plans, but he wants to offer us so much more than what we would give ourselves. God's plans account for every minuscule detail, weaving every strand of history and every moment of individual lives into a tapestry that depicts the grandest story of love. What might we discover is in store for us when we allow ourselves to let God shape the design?

God, I praise you for your great and glorious plans.

Sit in silence with the Lord.

Make a basic timeline of important "God moments" in your life. Reflect on how God's plan for you has unfolded over the years.

**† Lord, I give myself over to your plan. "The LORD knows the plans
of man; they are like a fleeting breath." Amen.**

Palm Sunday

† **Wait for the Lord, whose salvation draws near.**

"All who see me scoff at me; they mock me with parted lips, they wag their heads" (Ps 22:8).

Today we commemorate the day Jesus rode into Jerusalem to shouts of praise. Just a few days later, all who saw him would scoff at him, mock him with parted lips, and shake their heads as he carried his Cross through the same streets. In each case, the crowds stopped life in the city to mark Jesus passing by. Some joined in the processions. Some simply stopped to watch. Others, I would imagine, were inconvenienced by the spectacle or perhaps fearful of what might happen to their neighborhoods and homes because of this would-be Messiah.

As we move into Holy Week, let us pause a minute to consider where we might find ourselves in the crowd as Christ passes by. Do we join in? Do we simply stop and watch? Do we see Jesus's presence as an inconvenience, keeping us from taking care of the things on our to-do lists? Do we minister to him? Or do we fear that Jesus's presence means everything is about to change dramatically? Are we frightened?

This Holy Week, Jesus will be passing by. How will we meet him on the way?

Lord, open my heart to your presence.

Sit in silence with the Lord.

As we enter into the holiest days of our year, ask the Holy Spirit to help you be present to the saving work of Jesus in his Passion, Death, and Resurrection.

† **Lord Jesus, help me stop and see you in the midst of this Holy Week. I want to know you, Lord. "All who see me scoff at me; they mock me with parted lips, they wag their heads." Amen.**

Monday of Holy Week

† **Wait for the Lord, whose salvation draws near.**

"Wait for the LORD with courage; be stouthearted, and wait for the LORD" (Ps 27:14).

Holy Week is a week to wait for the Lord. Activity around our churches slows down and we focus solely on the Passion, Death, and Resurrection of Our Lord. The stillness is both foreign and familiar. And it forces us to wait even if we don't want to.

Lean into the stillness of this week. When the fasting gets wearisome, when knees ache from kneeling, take a deep breath and wait for the Lord. While our waiting may not require as much courage as Jesus showed, our discipline refines us to be able to bear harder things. Be stouthearted in the small moments, when the temptation is to skip the sad parts of Jesus's story and go straight to the celebration. We cannot have the Resurrection without the Crucifixion. We must go through Golgotha to find the empty tomb.

Wait for the Lord with courage; be stouthearted and wait for the Lord.

Thank you, Lord, for the waiting.

Sit in silence with the Lord.

Spend one or two minutes in silent stillness. Try to resist any distractions and simply be with God.

† **Lord, help me wait upon you, for your salvation is my joy. "Wait for the LORD with courage; be stouthearted, and wait for the LORD." Amen.**

Tuesday of Holy Week

"My mouth shall declare your justice, day by
day your salvation" (Ps 71:15).

One great gift of Holy Week is its bold and unashamed proclamation of the Good News of salvation. Our mouths declare God's justice as we share the stories of the Paschal Mystery. Day by day God's salvation is recounted as we celebrate the sacrifice of Our Lord. This week is a gift to each of us as we remember what the Lord has done for us. And it is a gift to the world because it testifies to the profound meaning of the life, death, and Resurrection of Jesus for every person.

The challenge we receive in Holy Week is to not forget the Good News of salvation and to share it with others day by day. We are invited to declare to a world desperate for justice that God has redeemed the world and a new kingdom of love and justice is breaking out here and now. Holy Week may confidently recount the Paschal Mystery, but it is our witness to the gospel that allows others to experience the saving power of Christ in their everyday lives.

Lord Jesus, show me how to witness to the Good News.

Sit in silence with the Lord.

Come up with a short description of the gospel message and think about how you would share it with a friend.

† **May I proclaim your salvation, Lord, to all who would hear your voice. "My mouth shall declare your justice, day by day your salvation." Amen.**

Wednesday of Holy Week

† Wait for the Lord, whose salvation draws near.

"For your sake I bear insult, and shame covers my face" (Ps 69:8).

Jesus bore insult and pain for our sake. The shame of his torture covered him literally in scars. His hands and feet were pierced. Blood and water flowed from his side. He saw his mother and his friends weeping for him. He heard the mocking taunts as his strength slowly ebbed. He spent his very last breath on a Roman cross. And he bore it all for us.

What are we willing to bear for Jesus in turn? Are we willing to confront insults and shame? Or do we stay in our comfort zone, keeping our faith private and personal when it's inconvenient or embarrassing? What crosses are we willing to take up for the Lord, and which would we try to set aside? More importantly, how might this Holy Week give us the courage to accept our crosses as Jesus accepted his and bear witness to God's abundant grace?

Thank you, Jesus, for all you bore for my sake.

Sit in silence with the Lord.

Identify one of the "crosses" in your life. Ask God to help you carry it this week.

† Give me courage, Lord, to bear even insult for your name. "For your sake I bear insult, and shame covers my face." Amen.

Holy Thursday

† Wait for the Lord, whose salvation draws near.

"How shall I make a return to the LORD for all the good he has done for me?" (Ps 116:12).

How shall I make a return to the Lord for all he has done for me? How could I ever repay God for the victory that Jesus accomplished on the Cross in my stead? What praise could I ever give which would be enough to honor Christ for giving me his very Body and Blood in the Eucharist? I will never be able to do enough to show the Triune God how thankful I am. I have nothing good enough to offer the Lord.

Yet God does not expect us to repay his merciful kindness. He instead gives us even greater gifts through our offerings, which become sacrAmen.ts of his grace. The Lord takes the simplest things we *can* offer—water, oil, bread, wine—and gives us God's very life through them. What a generous friend we have in Jesus! He doesn't need anything we have but gives us everything we could ever possibly need.

Thank you, God, for giving me your grace.

Sit in silence with the Lord.

If possible, go to the Mass of the Lord's Supper at your parish this evening. Contemplate the meaning of the Washing of the Feet at this opening of the Paschal Triduum.

† Thank you, Jesus, for all you have done for me. Thank you for giving me everything I need. "How shall I make a return to the LORD for all the good he has done for me?" Amen.

April 18

Good Friday

† Wait for the Lord, whose salvation draws near.

"I say, 'You are my God. In your hands is my destiny; rescue me from the clutches of my enemies and my persecutors'" (Ps 31:15b–16).

In your hand is my destiny, Lord. You have knit me in my mother's womb and numbered each one of my days. Rescue me from the ways I sabotage my own holiness and the sins I cannot seem to let go. Save me from the enemies of selfishness, addiction, and cynicism. Keep me from the persecutors of oppression, injustice, abuse, aggression, hopelessness, and indifference. Do not let me fall into their clutches, but shelter me within your holy presence.

Let me live in imitation of Jesus, who trusted that you kept his destiny within your hands. Give me the courage he had during his Crucifixion to resist the temptation to despair and believe that his death would not be in vain. Help me to trust in your great power over sin and death. Most of all, thank you for your victory accomplished through the Cross of Jesus. You have defeated every unseen enemy of human flourishing, and we rejoice in knowing our destiny is safe in your hands.

I adore you, O Christ, and I praise you for your saving, holy Cross.

Sit in silence with the Lord.

Keep one minute of solemn silence to honor the Lord's Passion.

† Father, help me to trust you like Jesus did. "But my trust is in you, O LORD; I say, 'You are my God. In your hands is my destiny; rescue me from the clutches of my enemies and my persecutors.'" Amen.

Holy Saturday

† Wait for the Lord, whose salvation draws near.

"You will not abandon my soul to the netherworld, nor will you suffer your faithful one to undergo corruption" (Ps 16:10).

God will not abandon our souls to the netherworld, nor will God suffer his faithful ones to undergo corruption. On this night, Jesus himself descended into the netherworld in order that we would not have to experience any separation from God. God could not tolerate the thought of having any one of us apart from the Divine Presence. God never intended for there to be decay, corruption, or any victory for sin and death over his beloved children. And so, Jesus remedied that corruption by going into the depths of Sheol himself.

This unimaginable gift of new life is a divine love letter to each of us. The thing that no human can defeat—death itself—has been conquered by Our Lord *for us*. Christ didn't do it simply because he could. He did it because he sees each of us as infinitely precious and worth any sacrifice. Jesus saw what we could not do ourselves and did it willingly instead. Let us remember today how beloved we are as we wait in joyful hope for the celebration of his glorious Resurrection.

Lord, I stand in awe of how much you love me.

Sit in silence with the Lord.

Is there anything that keeps you from fully accepting the love of God in Christ Jesus? Tell God what barriers you need removed.

† God, I thank you for defeating sin and death. You are worthy of all praise. "You will not abandon my soul to the netherworld, nor will you suffer your faithful one to undergo corruption." Amen.

April 20
Easter Sunday

† **This is the day the Lord has made, Let us rejoice and be glad!**

"The stone which the builders rejected has become the cornerstone"
(Ps 118:22).

Rejoice and be glad! Jesus, Our Lord and Savior, has risen from the grave and he will never die again! The stone that the builders rejected has become the cornerstone of faith, hope, and mercy for all time. God has overturned the reign of sin and death, taking what was despised and lowly and making it the foundation of a kingdom of compassion and grace. Jesus is bringing a reign of gentleness and peace that is turning the world upside down.

Where will the joy of the Resurrection lead you in the Easter season? How is Christ calling you to continue to grow in relationship with him? What ways will you advance God's upside-down kingdom in your relationships? In your community? In our nation? In the world?

The Lord's salvation is not far away from us. It is here and now. The joy of the Resurrection is for me and you, and it can turn the world upside down. Alleluia!

Sit in silence with the Lord.

Rest in the presence of Jesus and revel in the joy of salvation.

† **Thank you, Lord, for turning the world upside down. I will glorify you forever! "The stone which the builders rejected has become the cornerstone." Amen. Alleluia!**

Acknowledgments

Writing a devotional has been a secret hope of mine for many years, and it's a true joy to see this little work in print. There are so many people to thank for making it a reality, so apologies for only acknowledging a few!

First and foremost, thanks to my lovely editor, Eileen Ponder, for bringing this project to my figurative doorstep. I'm also eternally grateful to all the staff at Ave Maria Press who are a joy to work with as an author.

I'd also like to thank my family for their love and patience as I took on yet another writing project. Special thanks to my kids, Owen, Will, Molly, and Megan, who ate one too many frozen pizzas because I was too tired to make dinner after writing.

Above all, I am grateful to my God, who loves me beyond measure and in spite of all the ways I fall short. May this small offering give you glory and testify to your abundant grace!

Shannon Wimp Schmidt is the content director of the ecumenical youth ministry collaboration TENx10, coauthor of *Fat Luther, Slim Pickin's: A Black Catholic Celebration of Faith, Tradition*, and *Diversity*, cohost of the *Plaid Skirts and Basic Black* podcast, and a founding member of Catholics United for Black Lives.

Schmidt earned a bachelor's degree in theology and Italian from the University of Notre Dame and a master's degree in pastoral studies from Catholic Theological Union. She has more than a decade of experience in youth and pastoral ministry and has served in various capacities, including director of OCIA, adult faith formation coordinator, diversity educator, interfaith ministry leader, and theology teacher.

Schmidt's work has been featured in Fem Catholic, *U.S. Catholic Magazine*, the *Catholic Standard*, the National Catholic Reporter, and on CatholicTV's *This Is the Day*.

She lives with her husband and their four children near Chicago, Illinois.

psbbpodcast.com

X: @teamquarterblk

Instagram: @teamquarterblack